STARK LIBRARY

Dinosaurs
Pteranodon

by Julie Murray

Dash!
LEVELED READERS

An Imprint of Abdo Zoom • abdobooks.com

Dash!
LEVELED READERS

Level 1 – Beginning
Short and simple sentences with familiar words or patterns for children who are beginning to understand how letters and sounds go together.

Level 2 – Emerging
Longer words and sentences with more complex language patterns for readers who are practicing common words and letter sounds.

Level 3 – Transitional
More developed language and vocabulary for readers who are becoming more independent.

THIS BOOK CONTAINS RECYCLED MATERIALS

abdobooks.com

Published by Abdo Zoom, a division of ABDO, PO Box 398166, Minneapolis, Minnesota 55439.
Copyright © 2023 by Abdo Consulting Group, Inc. International copyrights reserved in all countries.
No part of this book may be reproduced in any form without written permission from the publisher.
Dash!™ is a trademark and logo of Abdo Zoom.

Printed in the United States of America, North Mankato, Minnesota.
052022
092022

Photo Credits: Alamy, Getty Images, Science Source, Shutterstock
Production Contributors: Kenny Abdo, Jennie Forsberg, Grace Hansen, John Hansen
Design Contributors: Candice Keimig, Neil Klinepier

Library of Congress Control Number: 2021950315

Publisher's Cataloging in Publication Data

Names: Murray, Julie, author.
Title: Pteranodon / by Julie Murray
Description: Minneapolis, Minnesota : Abdo Zoom, 2023 | Series: Dinosaurs | Includes online resources and index.
Identifiers: ISBN 9781098228286 (lib. bdg.) | ISBN 9781098229122 (ebook) | ISBN 9781098229542 (Read-to-Me ebook)
Subjects: LCSH: Pteranodon--Juvenile literature. | Dinosaurs--Juvenile literature. | Paleontology--Juvenile literature. | Extinct animals--Juvenile literature.
Classification: DDC 567.90--dc23

Table of Contents

Pteranodon 4

More Facts 22

Glossary 23

Index 24

Online Resources 24

Pteranodon was a large flying reptile called a Pterosaur. It lived 75 million years ago.

Pteranodon was not a dinosaur. But it lived among the dinosaurs.

It stood six feet (1.8 m) tall. It weighed 35 pounds (15.9 kg).

Pteranodon had a big head with a crest.

It had three fingers on each hand. Each foot had four toes.

12

Pteranodon had a long beak. It did not have teeth. It used its beak to hunt.

15

17

Pteranodon had giant wings. It had a **wingspan** of 25 feet (7.6 m)!

19

It **soared** high in the sky. It dove down to scoop up fish. It ate them whole.

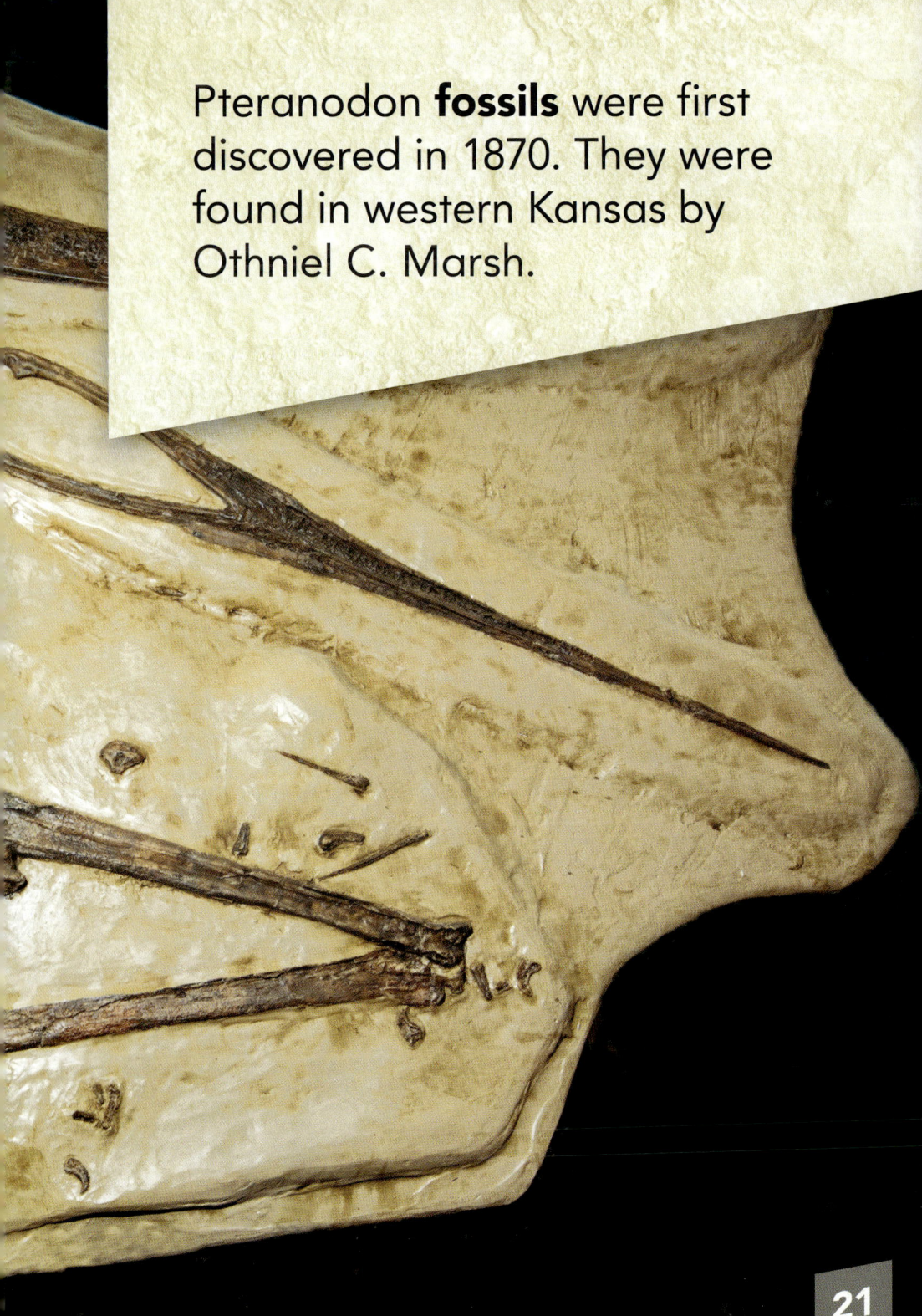

Pteranodon **fossils** were first discovered in 1870. They were found in western Kansas by Othniel C. Marsh.

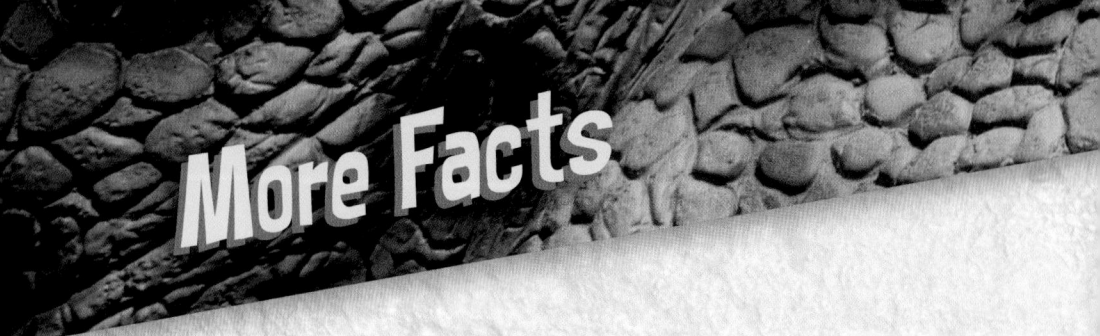

More Facts

- *Pteranodon* means "toothless wing."

- Males were larger than females. Their **crests** were larger too!

- Their heads and bodies may have been covered in fur.

Glossary

crest – a long tube projecting upwards from the back of the skull of some dinosaurs and ancient flying reptiles.

fossil – the remains or trace of a living animal or plant from a long time ago. Fossils are found embedded in earth or rock.

soar – to fly or glide in a swift, easy way.

wingspan – the distance from the tip of one wing to the tip of the other.

Index

beak 14

crest 10

feet 12

flying 17, 19

food 14, 19

fossils 21

hands 12

head 10

hunting 14, 19

Kansas 21

Marsh, Othniel C. 21

size 8

weight 8

wings 17

Online Resources

Booklinks
NONFICTION NETWORK
FREE! ONLINE NONFICTION RESOURCES

To learn more about Pteranodon, please visit **abdobooklinks.com** or scan this QR code. These links are routinely monitored and updated to provide the most current information available.